THE SIAMESE KITTENS AND THE SNOW LEOPARD

Also by Michael Haykin & Chris Iliff
Reformation Lightning

The Siamese Kittens and the Breadcrumbs
The Siamese Kittens and the Christmas Hedgehog

THE
SIAMESE KITTENS
AND THE
SNOW LEOPARD

Michael A.G. Haykin
Illustrated by Chris Iliff

Reformation
Lightning

Copyright © 2023 by Michael A.G. Haykin

First published in Great Britain in 2023

British Library Cataloguing in Publication Data
A record for this book is available from the British Library

ISBN: 978-1-916669-00-0

Designed and typeset by Pete Barnsley (CreativeHoot.com)
Illustrated by Chris Iliff (ChrisIliff.co.uk)

Printed in Denmark

Reformation Lightning, an imprint of 10Publishing
Unit C, Tomlinson Road, Leyland, PR25 2DY, England

Email: info@10ofthose.com
Website: www.10ofthose.com

1 3 5 7 10 8 6 4 2

I

HOLIDAYS

Do you like the Christmas holidays? They aren't as long  as other holidays. There is often snow on the ground and it is colder, and the days are shorter. But there is all the fun of Christmas presents, carols, mince pies, and family coming to visit.

Our Siamese kittens – do you remember their names? Java, Siam, and Ko-ko – well, they *loved* the Christmas holidays. They especially loved the Christmas tree with all its twinkly lights. There were green lights and red ones, blue lights, yellow ones and even a few purple ones. And of course, there were plenty of white lights.

The kittens would sit – it seemed for hours – simply watching the lights sparkling and twinkling, all of the colours reflecting on the wall – a bit like a rainbow.

The Quinns would put their presents out under the Christmas tree a few days before Christmas. And when they went to bed, the kittens had great fun pulling at the paper wrapping, even biting and eating the bows and ribbons. They weren't interested in seeing what was inside. They could smell it wasn't food and therefore it was of no real interest to them. They were just being kittens.

When the Quinns would come down in the morning, they would have to re-wrap some of the presents.

"Which one of you did this?" they would ask the kittens.

They usually figured it was either Ko-ko or Siam, both of whom could be quite naughty at times. Ko-ko was a great climber and Siam loved nothing better than an adventure. But the kittens pretended as if they had not heard the question and simply refused to admit to being naughty.

(Of course, if you or I are naughty, we should always admit it and say we're sorry.)

This year, one of the Quinn children, Lucy, received a backpack as her Christmas present. But it wasn't just any backpack. According to the online store where Mr Quinn bought it,

this backpack was designed for the *felis catus*, which is a Latin term for our word "cat."

Lucy couldn't contain her joy. She loved the Siamese kittens and now she could take them out with her whenever she went to visit her friends or her granny.

The backpack was a lovely turquoise colour with side pockets for treats and mesh windows so that the kitten inside could breathe easily. It also had a small opening at the top so the kitten could poke his or her head out and see what was happening.

"There's more," Mr Quinn said with a smile. He explained how they had decided to take the Quinn children – the Quinnlings, their parents sometimes called them – to the Dublin zoo as a Christmas treat to see the snow leopard Ciara and her two new little cubs.

2

THE CAT
CARRIER

So, the Quinns were going to take one of the Siamese kittens to the zoo in the cat carrier.

But who to take?

Since it was Lucy's backpack, they let her decide.

Well, said Lucy, Ko-ko loved to climb so she was afraid that Ko-ko would manage to climb out of the backpack and run off. Her mother agreed. Then, Siam could be equally naughty and there was nothing that she loved more than an adventure. So, she too might try to escape. So, in the end, Lucy settled on Java. Her mother agreed.

But to make sure that Java was comfortable in the cat carrier, Lucy decided to test it out. She began to take Java everywhere: to the store, the park, the town, even to the Quinnlings' granny's house.

At first, though, Java really did not like it. In fact, he hated it. All that motion of being jolted around when Lucy was walking made him feel sick.

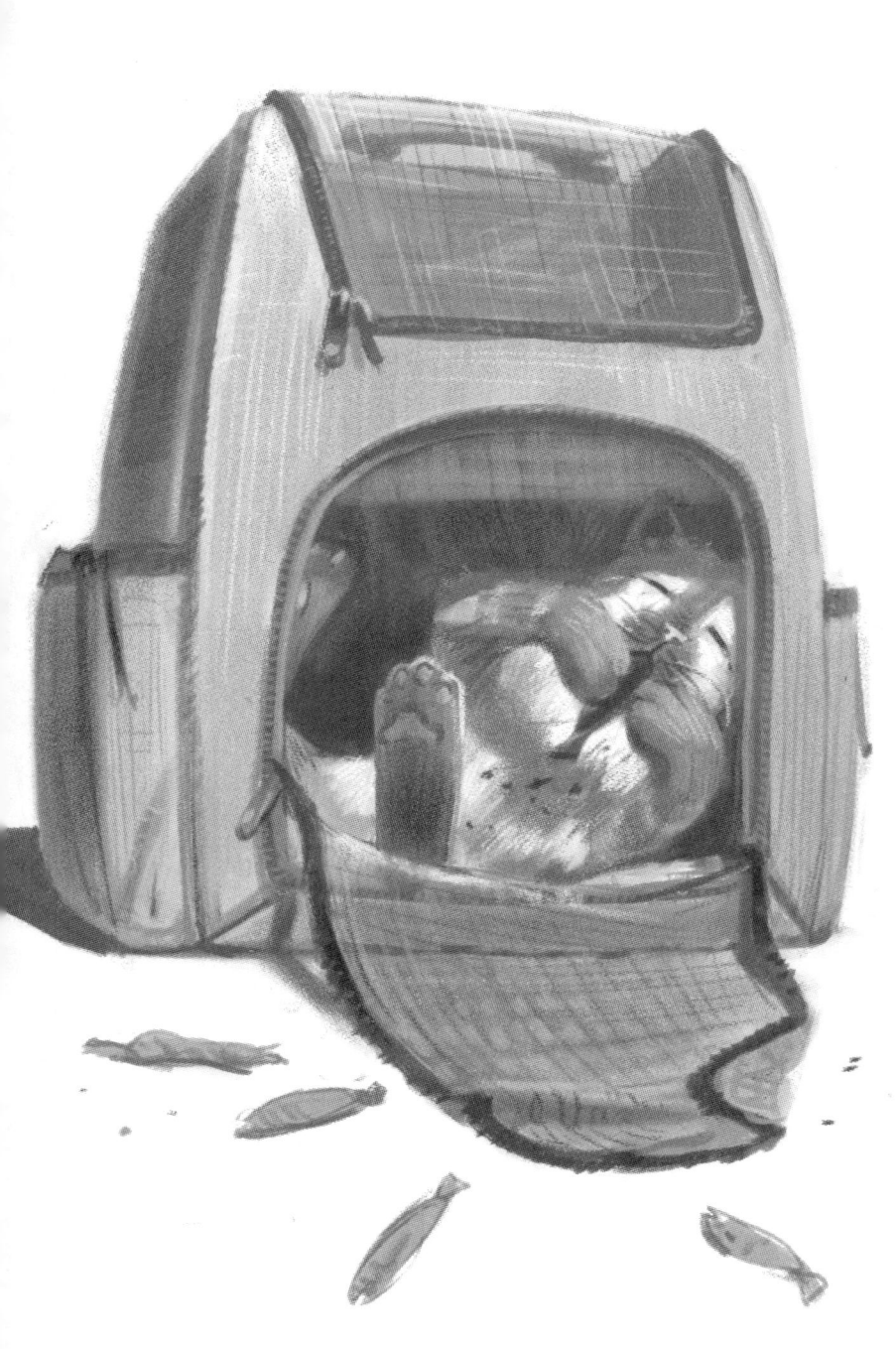

He was also really scared of where they might be going. When he was a very young kitten, only eight weeks old or so, the Quinns had taken him and his sisters to the vet to have their vaccinations against cat diseases. And they had carried the Siamese kittens in a pet carrier. He didn't like going to the vet, even though it was good for him.

But the space inside the cat backpack was quite small and cosy, and that made him feel good. And when he realised that he could smell fish treats in one of the outside pockets of the carrier, he liked it even more.

What a great way to travel, Java thought!

3

THE ZOO

The day that the Quinns planned to go to the zoo, there was a light dusting of snow on the ground. But it was a bright blue sky with not a cloud to be seen. Quite unusual for an Irish winter.

Lucy wanted to jump around with excitement. She picked up Java to put him into her backpack and the young kitten let out a small

squeak!

He was excited too – he couldn't wait to see the other big cats and show that he was just like them. (You may remember that Java was a ginger-coloured cat with furry orange stripes on his forehead and that he sometimes liked to pretend he was a tiger.)

He was also excited to ride in the backpack once again, especially as the backpack meant treats. But he had no idea of the real treat that was in store for him!

The Dublin Zoo is a great zoo. Java was amazed by how big the Asian elephants were, and thrilled by how tall the giraffes were.

The silverback gorillas amused Java with their antics. Well, Java *was* amused until one of the gorillas picked up a pebble and threw it at him. Nasty gorilla, he thought as Lucy walked away. She was eager to find Ciara the snow leopard and her cubs.

On their way, they found animals that Java heard Lucy call "meerkats". Java pricked his ears, expecting to find creatures like him.

But all Java saw when they came to the enclosure was twelve upright weaselly-looking animals staring up into the air with their paws bent. Java had no idea what they were looking at; when he looked up, he saw only the blue sky. Silly animals, Java thought. They should not be called "kats." They gave real cats a bad name.

They did see some real cats though, and big ones at that. First, there were the Asian lions. Well, Java didn't actually see them. The sign at the lion enclosure said they were there, but they must have all been sleeping in the lion den. Java then realized it was the afternoon, when normally he and his sisters also loved to have a long nap. But he was wide awake.

Finally, they came across the Amur tigers. When he saw one of the tigers yawn a big yawn with all his massive teeth showing, it inspired him again to think that he was like a tiger. Of course, there was a difference in size: tigers are the biggest cats in the world. Far, far bigger than our little Java. But that didn't matter, Java thought. He could be just

as fierce. He tried to r○a̲r̲ like a tiger to prove that he could indeed be one.

If his sisters had been there, they would have told him to stop being so silly. But they weren't there, and Java continued for a while pretending he was the fiercest Amur tiger in the world.

4

THE SNOW LEOPARDS

To Lucy's delight, they finally arrived at the snow leopards. Ciara had given birth to two female baby cubs a few months earlier. One of them was called "Mylo," which means "gracious," because the cub seemed to be very gentle. The other had an Irish name, Bán, which means "white," because, unlike her mother and sister who had the typical silver, white and black fur of snow leopards, she was very, very white. Lucy told Java their names, but he found them hard to say. Can you say them?

Ciara   Mylo   Bán

But what amazed Java the most were the eyes of all three snow leopards: they were pale green. He and his sisters (and Chai, the older cat in the Quinn house) were all Siamese cats with deep blue eyes. Java had never seen a cat with such pale green eyes. He was mesmerized.

Ciara was lying down, her big woolly tail wrapped around her body like a scarf, keeping herself warm. Her two cubs were playing beside her, jumping on her, and rolling off for fun. Mylo was especially playful. He even went over to their water bowl and began dunking his food in it and generally making a real mess. Now, that might be cool to do, Java thought to himself. Of course, this might be okay for cats like Java and leopards like Mylo to do, but please don't follow their example!

Lucy wanted to take some pictures of the snow leopards with her mobile, but her phone was in one of the pockets of the backpack. She took it off and began rummaging around to find it. Then she put her backpack down on the ground very close to the enclosure fence. In fact, Java's face was right up against the fence. He had a great view of the snow leopard cubs and stared at them bravely, in full tiger-mode.

Noticing him, the two cubs stopped what they were doing and tilted their heads. And with a speed that almost made Java jump, they began to bound over to the fence. They tried to talk to him, but he couldn't understand what they were saying. It sounded like a foreign language. It was cat talk, but they had a very thick accent. Of course, snow leopards don't come from Ireland, even though Mylo and Bán had been born there. Originally, snow leopards come from the mountains of Central Asia in China and India and Nepal and Mongolia (I wonder if you can find those countries on a map!).

So, their words sounded very funny to Java's ears – like they were talking through their noses. Of course, Java did not know that snow leopards have wide noses that help to take in deep breaths of air since they have to breathe very high up in the mountains where the air is thin.

What did they say to Java?

Well, what do you say when you have met someone for the first time?

"My name is Bán,"

the almost-completely white snow
leopard said.

"And my name is Mylo,"

squeaked the other.

But before Java could reply, the mother snow leopard noticed that her cubs were at the fence and became concerned for their safety. She roused herself and leapt over to the fence in a single bound. Wow! Was Java's first thought. What a huge jump! The wind rushed over him as she landed. She seemed so big, not as big as the lions or tigers, but still much bigger than him, with enormous furry paws.

For the first time that day, Java began to be afraid.

5

"WERE YOU AFRAID?"

"Were you afraid?" Ko-ko and Siam asked Java when he got home from the zoo and after he told them of his meeting with Ciara the snow leopard.

Java had expected the mother leopard to roar at him. But snow leopards cannot roar. Instead, she only let out a deep puffing sound that came as she blew breath out through her broad nose. Though Java had never heard such a sound before – it is called a chuff – he knew immediately that Ciara wasn't angry; she was saying hello and expressing love.

Java was no longer scared, but he was still afraid in a way he had never felt before. He couldn't look into Ciara's pale green eyes, his legs felt like jelly, and he was almost paralysed – in fact, the only part of him that could move was his neck.

And so, before that snow leopard, Java bowed his orangey-coloured head. He had a sudden and strong understanding that he really was

just a small Siamese cat – not a king and not a
tiger after all. And that was just right.

The two cats stayed like that for a long while, until Lucy realised what was happening and scooped Java and the backpack into her arms with a squeak.

"Were you afraid?" Ko-ko and Siam asked Java again.

"No, of course not," their brother insisted. But then, Java admitted, "Well yes, in a way. She was so big and majestic I couldn't help but feel afraid. I could feel her breath on my fur. But it wasn't like being scared. It was a nice sort of fear."

Siam and Ko-Ko looked confused.

"You'll have to meet her to understand." Java smiled.

Java never forgot the day he met Ciara the snow leopard. And for some reason, he never could imagine himself as a tiger again. But that didn't stop him trying to produce a chuff every now and then – though he never quite managed it through his fine pink nose!

"The fear of the Lord is the beginning
of wisdom,
and the knowledge of the Holy One
is understanding."

Proverbs 9:10

Read more *Siamese Kittens* from Ref Light:

Reformation Lightning

Kids fiction from a biblical worldview

We create thrilling stories that point to the greatest gospel story, giving truth a clear avenue into kids' hearts and imaginations.

Reformation Lightning is an imprint of 10Publishing and its titles are available through **10ofthose.com**